THE WORLD OF NASCAR

FANTASTIC FINISHES: NASCAR's Great Races

T R A D I T I O N   B O O K S®
A New Tradition in Children's Publishing™
MAPLE PLAIN, MINNESOTA

BY JIM GIGLIOTTI

Published by **Tradition Books®** and distributed to the
school and library market by **The Child's World®**
P.O. Box 326
Chanhassen, MN 55317-0326
800/599-READ
http://www.childsworld.com

Photo Credits
Cover: AP/Wide World
AP/Wide World: 5, 6, 10, 11, 13, 14, 15, 19, 25, 26, 27, 28
Corbis: 7, 8, 17, 20, 21
International Motorsports Hall of Fame: 16
Ken Coles: 23

An Editorial Directions book
Editorial Directions, Inc.: E. Russell Primm, Editorial Director; Katie Marsico and Elizabeth K.
Martin, Assistant Editors; Olivia Nellums, Editorial Assistant; Susan Hindman, Copy Editor;
Susan Ashley, Proofreader; Kevin Cunningham, Fact Checker; Tim Griffin/IndexServ, Indexer;
James Buckley Jr., Photo Researcher and Selector

Design Lab: Kathy Petelinsek, Art Director and Designer; Kari Thornborough,
Page Production

Library of Congress Cataloging-in-Publication Data
Gigliotti, Jim.
  Fantastic finishes : NASCAR's great races / by Jim Gigliotti.
    p. cm. — (World of NASCAR)
Summary: Reviews several NASCAR races that are memorable for the drivers, the
competitiveness, and/or the tactical maneuvering that made them exciting. Includes biblio-
graphical references and index.
  ISBN 1-59187-029-1 (library bound : alk. paper)
  1. Stock car racing—United States—History—Juvenile literature. 2. NASCAR
(Association)—Juvenile literature. [1. Stock car racing—History. 2. Automobile racing
drivers. 3. NASCAR (Association)] I. Title. II. Series.
GV1029.9.S74 G53 2003
796.72—dc21   2003008446

Note: Beginning with the 2004 season, the NASCAR
Winston Cup Series will be called the NASCAR Nextel
Cup Series.

F A N T A S T I C   F I N I S H E S

Table of Contents

INTRODUCTION

Fantastic Start

In 1959, a dream came true for NASCAR founder Bill France Sr. His stock cars moved from the sands of Daytona Beach, Florida, to the asphalt of the new Daytona International Speedway. The Daytona 500, which quickly became the most important race on the schedule, was born.

Not even in France's wildest dreams, though, did he expect the first Daytona 500 to end so memorably. Lee Petty and Johnny Beauchamp raced to the finish line, side-by-side and pedal-to-the-metal. The finish was literally too close to call because Joe Weatherly's **lapped** car also crossed the finish line at about the same time. The view of the officials was blocked. At first, they named Beauchamp the winner. Three days later, after reviewing photos and TV

footage, NASCAR reversed course and said Petty won the race.
The margin of victory was about 24 inches (61 centimeters).

It's hard to believe that after 500 miles (804.5 kilometers)
of driving, only 24 inches (61 cm) could separate the winners.
It was a fantastic finish. The 1959 Daytona 500, however, was
just one of many fantastic finishes in NASCAR history. Some
of the others you'll find on the following pages.

**Lee Petty (No. 42) and Johnny Beauchamp kicked off
NASCAR history with a photo finish at the 1959
Daytona 500.**

The races included here are not always the closest races. Sometimes they're races that are memorable for pitting a variety styles and personalities. Sometimes they're memorable for their competitiveness. Or they're memorable for brilliant tactical maneuvering.

Remember, the list is entirely **subjective.** Your favorite races may not be the same as mine. That's the beauty of spectator sports. Everyone sees the same thing, but we all see it a little differently. These are my favorites.

Driving across the finish line under the checkered flag is the goal of every driver in every race. But there can be only one winner!

CHAPTER ONE

Pearson Limps Home

I magine the winner of the Daytona 500 inching across the finish line no faster than a car moving through a school zone. Actually, you don't have to imagine it. It really happened in 1976. David Pearson edged legendary Richard Petty that year In perhaps NASCAR's most fantastic finish ever.

Petty and Pearson engaged in some classic head-to-head duels throughout their racing careers. They are two of the greatest racers in NASCAR history. Both are members of the International Motorsports Hall of Fame. Petty's 200 race wins are more than any other

In the 1960s and 1970s, Richard Petty was NASCAR's biggest star.

8   Amid the smoke are two of NASCAR's top racers.
Richard Petty and David Pearson collided on the
final lap of the 1976 Daytona 500.

NASCAR driver. Pearson's 105 wins rank second. They finished one-two in an incredible 63 races in their careers. Pearson's most famous victory over Petty, the man they call "The King," was at the 1976 Daytona 500.

The two drivers swapped the lead back and forth the last 46 laps of the 200-lap race around the 2.5-mile (4-km) oval track. Petty was in front on the last lap when Pearson zoomed past on the **backstretch.** Petty immediately tried to take the lead back by diving to the inside to pass Pearson again.

Petty didn't get all the way past Pearson, though. The two cars were side by side briefly when they hit each other coming out of the final turn. "He went beneath me and his car broke loose," Pearson said. "I got into the wall and came off and hit him. That's what started all the spinning."

Petty spun wildly backwards, toward the finish line at first, then down toward the **infield** just short of the finish line. Pearson started off spinning toward the infield and hit another car. The second collision sent him spinning back toward the

track. He had the presence of mind all the while, though, to engage the **clutch.** That way, he kept the motor running.

Pearson wanted to know if the race was over. Had Petty already crossed the finish line? His crew radioed that Petty hadn't reached the line, that he was stuck on the infield. "The King" was just 50 yards (46 meters) from the finish, but his car couldn't move. So Pearson put the pedal of his damaged car to the floor. He was going as fast as he could when his mangled car took the **checkered flag**—but it was only about 20 miles (32 km) per hour. "It seemed like I was a mile from the line and that it took forever to get there," he said.

It was an unbelievable finish. Petty had tried desperately to restart his engine as Pearson neared the finish line. He couldn't get his car started in time, and he finished second. Pearson won the Daytona 500 for the first and only time in his career.

Believe it or not, David Pearson steered this smashed-up car across the finish line to win the Daytona 500.

CLEVER LIKE A FOX

David Pearson edged Richard Petty in another fantastic finish at the Firecracker 400 in 1974. In that race, he did it with a bit of trickery down the final stretch.

Pearson led Petty on the final lap of the 160-lap race at Daytona. Pearson couldn't pull away from his rival, however, and he knew that second was the place to be. That's because if the driver in second place was close enough, he could sit in the **draft** of the car in front of him. Then the second-place car would "sling-shot" past the leader. This used to be the favored technique on fast tracks such as Daytona and Talladega.

Pearson wanted to be in second place going into the final turn. So he slowed down and moved his car to the left, toward the infield. Petty, the spectators, and the media all thought something was wrong with Pearson's car. Petty zoomed past. There was nothing wrong with Pearson's car, though. He quickly got back to speed and moved up behind Petty. Coming out of the last turn, Pearson shot past Petty and won by one car length.

Pearson's move was risky, but dramatic. It was the kind of maneuver that earned him the nickname "Silver Fox."

In 1984, Petty came out on top after another duel with Pearson.

CHAPTER TWO

Yarborough Is the Leader of the Pack

The Talladega Superspeedway is the fastest track on the NASCAR circuit. Before **restrictor plate** rules, drivers took advantage of the roomy oval track to slingshot past other cars. That helped to make some of the races at Talladega among the most exciting and competitive in NASCAR history. In fact, 6 of the 10 most competitive races in terms of lead changes came at Talladega. NASCAR's fastest qualifying time and its fastest 500-mile (804.5-km) race ever also were held at the track.

For sheer back-and-forth drama, it's hard to beat the 1984 Winston 500 at Talladega, which back then was known as the Alabama International Motor Speedway. "It was the

The action is always fast and furious at Talladega, one
of NASCAR's fastest tracks.

wildest race I've ever been in," Benny Parsons said. Cale Yarborough said, "It was amazing out there."

Parsons and Yarborough were 2 of the 13 different drivers who led the pack that afternoon in May. The 13 men passed the lead among them an astounding 75 times. That's a NASCAR record for a single race.

Yarborough trailed leader Harry Gant on the final lap. They roared down the backstretch with Yarborough nearly on Gant's bumper. Yarborough was one of the most successful drivers in NASCAR history

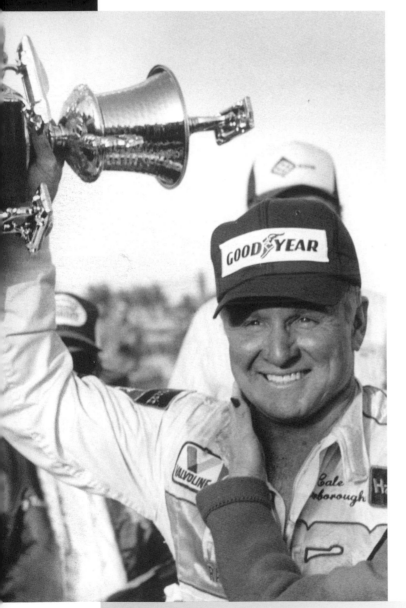

14 Cale Yarborough in a familiar pose: Holding up the winner's trophy after a NASCAR race in 1983.

at that time. His 83 career victories rank fifth on the all-time

list. He won three Winston Cup championships. Legendary

driver and car owner Junior Johnson called Yarborough

"the best driver the sport has ever seen." So Gant knew he

was in for a battle. He figured the slingshot was coming, but

he couldn't stop it. Yarborough zoomed past Gant and into

the lead.

Cale Yarborough's No. 27 car uses a slingshot move to zoom past Harry Gant to win the race!

THE HIGH ROAD

Less than three months after the 1984 Winston 500, Talladega (then called the Alabama International Motor Speedway) was the site of another fantastic finish. At the Talladega 500 in July, Dale Earnhardt Sr. outlasted the rest of the field to win—but it wasn't easy. Earnhardt had to rally from 23rd place with 13 laps to go. He called it "the most exciting race" he'd ever run.

Sixteen drivers exchanged the lead 68 times. On the next-to-last lap, 10 drivers still were bunched tightly together. Terry Labonte was in the lead, but each of the drivers had a chance to win. So Earnhardt decided he'd better do something to separate himself from the pack. Instead of dropping down on the track to pass Labonte, he decided to take the high road.

Coming out of the second turn, Earnhardt kept his car high on the track and stayed there. By the fourth turn, he had caught the leader on the outside and passed him heading into the final lap. From there, no one was going to catch the "Intimidator." He won by more than one second.

Dale Earnhardt Sr. hoisted the winner's trophy in 1984 at Talladega.

There was still enough of the final lap left for Gant to slingshot past Yarborough one last time, though. This time, Yarborough knew it was coming—but he got a little lucky. When Gant made his move, another car on the crowded track got in the way.

Gant settled back in behind Yarborough. Still, Yarborough wasn't home free. As he came out of the last turn, he was running out of gas. And it obviously wasn't the time or place for a **pit stop!** So he jostled the car gently from side to side to get the last ounce of gas from his tank. He crossed the finish line just two car lengths ahead of Gant. He averaged nearly 173 miles (276 km) per hour over the 188 laps of the race. That was another record at the time. After the race, Yarborough admitted that by the time he reached the finish line, he was running on fumes.

Cale Yarborough is dirty but happy in the winner's circle on Victory Lane.

C H A P T E R   T H R E E

The President and "The King"

It's hard to believe that one of the most exciting finishes to a NASCAR race actually came under the **yellow caution flag.** It's true, though. Here's how it happened.

In 1984, the Pepsi Firecracker 400 was held on July 4 at Daytona. It was a day filled with emotion. A huge crowd was on hand. It was Independence Day, and the fans hoped to see Richard Petty win the 200th race of his career. No one else had even come close to that number. Plus, President Ronald Reagan was going to be in attendance. It was the first time a sitting president of the United States had ever gone to a NASCAR race.

The president's plane was still on the way when the race started. So from a phone in the plane, Mr. Reagan called out the

Richard Petty roars to victory at the 1984 Firecracker 400. It was the 200th victory of his amazing career.

traditional words to start the race: "Gentlemen, start your engines!" Ninety minutes later, the sight of the president's plane landing while the race was in progress was incredible. The massive **Air Force One** touched down just outside the wall beyond Turn 2 as cars raced past.

The real drama came on the racetrack, though. Petty had won his 199th race in May at the Budweiser 500. This was his fifth try at number 200. After 157 laps of this 160-lap race at Daytona, Petty had a slight lead over Cale Yarborough. No

President Ronald Reagan watched from the stands during the 1984 Firecracker 400.

one else was close. It was evident that one of the two drivers would win.

There was a crash, however, on the 158th lap. Neither Petty nor Yarborough was involved, but the yellow caution flag came out. Under caution rules, drivers maintain the position they are in once they pass the flag stand. Other drivers slowed down once they had taken the yellow caution flag. Being far ahead, though, Petty and Yarborough passed the stand before the yellow flag came out. So they could keep racing until they passed the stand again.

Both drivers knew what was at stake. With only two-plus laps to go, the race was sure to end under the caution flag. So Petty and Yarborough floored it. They knew whoever led at the end of the 158th lap was going to be the winner of the race. It was a sprint to the lap line.

The two drivers dashed around the track. First, Yarborough shot past Petty's famous number 43 on the backstretch. Petty quickly moved to the inside and drew back

alongside Yarborough. It was door-to-door racing at its best. Petty and Yarborough flew toward the flag stand at nearly 200 miles (320 km) per hour. They bumped once, twice, three times. "The last 'bam' sort of squirted me ahead," Petty said.

That was just the edge he needed. Petty crossed the flag stand barely ahead of Yarborough. His 200th victory was secured. Because the race ended under caution two laps later, there is no official margin of victory credited. The actual margin, though, was about the width of a fender. That's how close it was when Petty and Yarborough crossed the lap line.

President Reagan told Petty after the race that he'd never seen anything like it. "The King" was **euphoric** that his record win came on July 4 with the president in attendance. "I couldn't have asked for a better time," Petty said.

The champagne was spraying as Richard Petty celebrated his 200th victory.

CLOSE CALLS

Many other famous NASCAR races have been as close as that 1984 Firecracker 400. Here are a couple of examples.

In 1980, Buddy Baker and Dale Earnhardt Sr. raced side-by-side to the finish of the Winston 500 at Talladega. They hurtled toward the checkered flag at more than 200 miles (320 km) per hour. Baker won by 36 inches (91 cm).

In 1990, Davey Allison bypassed a pit stop to take the lead three-quarters of the way through the Valleydale 500 in Bristol, Tennessee. Allison held the lead the rest of the way—but only barely. At the end, a hard-charging Mark Martin fell 6 inches (15.2 cm) short of winning. It was so close when the two cars crossed the finish line that officials couldn't name a winner right away. They had to watch videotape of the photo finish.

Dale Jarrett won his first career race at the Champion Spark Plug 400 in 1991. He cut it close, though, edging Davey Allison by just 10 inches (25 cm).

Dale Jarrett No. 21 battled Richard Petty No. 43 and then held off Davey Allison to win this 1991 NASCAR race.

C H A P T E R   F O U R

Gordon Holds Off the "Intimidator"

Ten laps from the end of the Daytona 500 in 1999, Jeff Gordon glanced up and saw legendary Dale Earnhardt Sr. in his rearview mirror. Earnhardt was so close it looked as if he was in Gordon's back seat. From that point to the finish, there was no letup in the action. The 27-year-old Gordon and the 47-year-old Earnhardt battled head to head. "It was intense and exciting from where I was sitting," Gordon said.

Gordon was sitting in the lead for the final 10 laps. He got there with a brilliant pass on the lap before. At that point, Gordon had been in third place, trailing Rusty Wallace and Earnhardt. When Earnhardt tried to pass Wallace, Gordon could have followed. Instead, he surprised everyone by dropping

down the track beside Earnhardt. He quickly passed Earnhardt
and went after Wallace himself.

Suddenly, Gordon saw Ricky Rudd ahead of him near the
bottom of the track. Rudd was a lap behind and moving slowly.
Gordon was moving very quickly. "Oh, Ricky, I hope you see
me coming because I'm coming real fast," Gordon said to himself. Gordon thought he might have to slam on the brakes.
Instead, a narrow opening appeared to the right of Rudd and
the left of Wallace. Gordon came right up to Rudd's bumper,
then darted through the opening and into first place.

The move was so bold and so intense, and the opening was
so small, that Gordon's wife, Brooke, screamed. She was watch-
ing on television inside their trailer on the infield. Jeff was safe,

The 1999 Daytona 500 is under way! Jeff Gordon
(front right) leads the way from the pole position.

though—and safely in the lead. Now he had to deal with Earnhardt, who came out of the **fray** in second place.

They didn't call Earnhardt the "Intimidator" for nothing. Earnhardt was one of the most aggressive drivers in the history of NASCAR. He thought nothing of bumping a car out of the way if it stood between him and the checkered flag. Earnhardt drove right up to Gordon's bumper. "I really thought he was going to get me," Gordon admitted.

Earnhardt couldn't get in position to nudge Gordon safely out of the way, though. So on each of the final 10 laps, Earnhardt tried to set up Gordon for a pass. He tried to pass right. He couldn't. He tried to pass left. He couldn't. He tried to get underneath Gordon in the turns. He couldn't. "I just never could get to him," Earnhardt said after the race. "It wasn't meant to be, I reckon."

Just feet in front of a hard-charging Dale Earnhardt, Jeff Gordon's No. 24 car races across the finish line at the 1999 Daytona 500.

Coming out of the final turn and heading for the checkered flag, Gordon felt a little bump from the Intimidator. It was just "a love tap," Gordon said. Luckily, it was nothing worse. The younger driver sprinted to the finish. He beat Earnhardt by just a car length.

For Gordon, winning the prestigious Daytona 500 for the second time was exhilarating. Holding off the Intimidator to do it made it even more special. "It's a dream come true for me to race Dale Earnhardt all the way to the finish line in the Daytona 500," he said.

Wooo-yeah! Jeff Gordon screams in celebration after climbing out of his car in Victory Lane as confetti falls around him.

THE GREAT AMERICAN RACE

It's no surprise that the Daytona 500, the biggest race on the schedule, has provided many of NASCAR's most fantastic finishes. The memories go back to the very first Daytona 500 in 1959 and include the great 1976 race in chapter 2.

In 1979, another last-lap crash knocked out leaders Davey Allison and Cale Yarborough. That enabled Richard Petty to race to the finish line with Darell Waltrip on his bumper. Allison and Yarborough, meanwhile, got into a fistfight on the infield.

In 1988, Bobby Allison beat his son Davey by two car lengths at the finish. It was the first and only time a father and son finished one-two at Daytona.

In 2001, Michael Waltrip held off Dale Earnhardt Jr. to win by about one-eighth of one second. Dale Earnhardt Sr. helped make the win possible by running interference for the two leaders on the last lap. The race ended in tragedy, though, when Earnhardt Sr. crashed in the last turn and was killed instantly.

Davey Allison and his father Bobby (right) battled to a one-two finish at the 1988 Daytona 500.

TIMELINE

1959   Lee Petty is officially named the winner of the inaugural Daytona 500 three days after the race is run

1974   David Pearson fakes car trouble and allows Richard Petty to pass him on the last lap of the Firecracker 400, setting up a late pass

1976   David Pearson limps across the finish line ahead of Richard Petty's stalled car after a last-lap crash in the Daytona 500

1979   Richard Petty wins the Daytona 500 while Davey Allison and Cale Yarborough brawl on the infield after a last-lap crash

1980   Buddy Baker outduels Dale Earnhardt Sr. in the Winston 500 at Talladega, winning by three feet (91 cm)

1984   On May 6, the lead changes hands 75 times in the Winston 500 at Talladega

On July 4, Richard Petty wins his 200th race, the Firecracker 400, with President Reagan in attendance

On July 29, the lead changes hands 68 times at the Talladega 500

1988   Father and son Bobby and Davey Allison finish one-two at the Daytona 500

1990   Davey Allison beats hard-charging Mark Martin by a mere 6 inches (15.2 cm) in the Valleydale 500 at Bristol, Tennessee

1991   Dale Jarrett wins his first Winston Cup race, the Champion Spark Plug 400, edging Davey Allison by just 10 inches (25 cm)

1999   Jeff Gordon holds off Dale Earnhardt Sr. to win the Daytona 500

2001   Michael Waltrip holds off Dale Earnhardt Jr. by .124 seconds to win the Daytona 500, but Dale Earnhardt Sr. is killed in a last-lap crash

GLOSSARY

Air Force One—the specially equipped plane that transported the president

backstretch—the straightaway opposite the side with the finish line

checkered flag—the flag that signifies the winning car has crossed the finish line

clutch—a device in a car that allows the driver to switch gears

disparate—distinct; different

draft—the vacuum created by the car in front that a trailing car uses to gain extra speed and conserve fuel

euphoric—extremely happy

fray—battle

infield—the portion of the racetrack inside the path formed by the roadway

lapped—when a car is a full lap behind the leaders and the leaders pass them again

pit stop—when a driver stops his car in mid-race for service, such as a tank of gas or a tire change

restrictor plate—a plate that restricts air and fuel flow to the carburetor, thus keeping speeds in check

subjective—based on personal feelings or opinions instead of facts

yellow caution flag—the flag that indicates there's trouble on the track; drivers are not allowed to pass other drivers once they've taken the yellow flag

FOR MORE INFORMATION ABOUT NASCAR RACING

Books

Barber, Phil. *Stock Car's Greatest Race: The First and the Fastest.* Excelsior, Minn.: Tradition Books, 2002.

Fleischman, Bill, and Al Pearce. *The Unauthorized NASCAR Fan Guide 2002.* Detroit: Visible Ink Press, 2002.

Frankl, Ron. *Richard Petty.* Broomall, Penn.: Chelsea House, 1996.

Higgins, Tom. *NASCAR Greatest Races: The Twenty-Five Most Thrilling Races in NASCAR History.* New York: HarperEntertainment, 1999.

Woods, Bob. *Dirt Track Daredevils: The History of NASCAR.* Excelsior, Minn: Tradition Books, 2002.

Web Sites

Daytona 500
http://www.daytona500.com
For complete racing results, a track map, and stories of great races

The Official Web Site of NASCAR
http://www.nascar.com
For information on famous races and drivers in NASCAR history, click on "Know Your NASCAR"

Videos

NASCAR's Greatest Races
Part of ESPN's NASCAR "Greatest" series, produced by Lingner Group Productions in association with ESPN

INDEX

ABOUT THE AUTHOR

Jim Gigliotti is a freelance writer who lives with his wife and two children in Westlake Village, California. He has worked for the University of Southern California athletic department, the Los Angeles Dodgers, and the National Football League. He has written biographies of Dale Jarrett and Jeff Gordon for The World of NASCAR series.